Nothing Here Is Wild, Everything Is Open

Contents

Acknowledgements

After the man who finds a 100-year-old bottle made by her great-grandfather's company, with his name still on it, won't sell it to her was published in *B O D Y*, October 2015.

The Biologist and the Birds was commended, 2014 Charles Causley Poetry Competition, and published online.

Conversations With a Taxi Driver, Falmouth, was first published in *Shearsman* magazine.

Hold The Baby was first published in *Butcher's Dog*, 2013.

Cultivation published in Winter 2015/16 issue of *The Stinging Fly*.

Delville Wood was commended in Magma's 2014 Editor's Prize and published in *Magma*, May 2014.

Dreams of a Tea Seller was shortlisted for the 2015 Live Canon Poetry Competition and published in the winners' anthology.

Lessons in Flanders Agriculture won 3rd prize in the inaugural Ruskin Poetry Competition 2015 and was published in *POEM* magazine.

The Observer Paradox was commended, 2014 Charles Causley Poetry Competition, and published online.

Pulled was commended, 2014 Ealing Autumn Festival Poetry Competition, and published online.

Enormous thanks to the following for their support, encouragement, workshops and inspiration on my journey towards poetry: Simon Armitage, Jeremy Banning, Miranda Barnes, Rachael Boast, Jo Bell, Marjorie Celona, Caroline Davis, Vanessa Gebbie, Pippa Goldschmidt, Sue Guiney, Melissa Lee-Houghton, Julie Maclean, Nuala O'Connor, Pascale Petit, Hilda Sheehan - and the Bristol poetry reading group, who open my eyes every month to so much new poetry: Helen Dunmore, Adam Elgar, Alison Elgar, Pat Ferguson, Ali Griffiths, Joe Melia and Helen Taylor.

For my dad,
who taught me how to solve a cryptic crossword,
which, it turns out, is very similar
to making a poem

And What We Know About Time

When it failed to alarm, my father
took the clock apart. Laid it
all out on the kitchen table. While the dog
dreamed and snored, we watched him
clean every piece, then, with breaths held,
attempt reassembly. It worked

perfectly for the next ten years, which was odd,
given the sixteen horological components
my father couldn't fit back in. (They
lived out their days in that kitchen drawer
designated for such things.)

There must have been someone, somewhere,
now - like my father, like the dog,
the kitchen table and that drawer -
long gone, who once knew
exactly what those sixteen parts were for.

Vandalism

Pieces which   when the glass was smashed
     slid into the innards of the door
now sing to me   of breakages
       and how a thing
once shattered
       may seem fixed

Hold The Baby

They said she had to hold the baby so she held the baby even though she had no notion why she held it, him or her. They said she couldn't look to see so in her mind she thought of it as both, a Jenny and a James, and she knew it wasn't right but there was nothing more to say. They said they'd run some tests while she was holding it, experiments of a sort, but she was not so clear what sort. Perhaps they measured angles, how she held it, how it sat there. Maybe they counted breaths, hers and its, or blood flow or pressure, with machines she couldn't see. Maybe they wired up her brain and knew what she was thinking, feeling. Some time had passed, maybe minutes, and she wanted to drop the baby. Not hard, not on the floor, just to not hold it any more.

Pulled

Once, early on in my development,
some boy took me to a roof
to see Orion's Belt, the Pleiades.

I listened, looked politely
where he pointed, but already then
I knew – although he'd left the door

ajar and I was not yet fully-
formed – that this had nothing
to do with stars, the tug of gravity.

Dreams Of A Tea Seller

I sell you teas: Lapsang
Souchong and Darjeeling
Oolong and Lady Grey.
                                    But
I want to be a builder,
I want to mix cement. Fuck

the scent of bergamot, the steeping
and the straining. I want to lay

foundations for the tallest buildings
                              and the smallest houses.
I want to wear builder's trousers
and a hard hat. I want not to be
fat and sat amongst the kettles

but sleek on building sites
with the foreman and his crew, muscled
and unbowing to any customer.

I want to swing from a girder
dropping my teapots
                    one by one
while drinking builder's brew, too milky
                        and too sweet for you.

Conversations With A Taxi Driver, Falmouth

Mirabella's mast, the world's largest, he tells me,
holds inside its vastness: stairs. No more scaling
rigging, a civilized ascent. Mirabella's mast, he
tells me, is made of lead, and we don't know, he
says, why it is so tall. Just because it can be. A
son, he tells me, drives around a General; he's an
army man. David, he says, David is treated well.
I imagine, as we go, the son, inside Mirabella's
mast, leading his General by the hand. Where is
my command? says the old man. Here, whispers
David.

Lessons In Flanders Agriculture

Folding a field takes an army
        one man at each corner
                many down the sides

They bend   slide their hands beneath
        chalk and sod   lift   and run
                towards their comrades

When it is done   when the light
        is gone   the men are spent   no-one
               is left to listen to the field   sighing

Delville Wood

From when they began
to when they ended
it was a moment's
sigh and droop. It was
a cuckoo's cry. It was
a horse
          Fire on them

A horse
          Fire on them!

A horse, grazing.

The Biologist And The Birds

It is her bedroom window
the birds fly into and fly

into, trying to get through.
It happens only in daylight

though she worries in the night, after
gently burying so many fallen bodies.

It seems to stop when she moves
her full-length mirror to another corner

of the room. Perhaps it was the apparent
patch of sky the birds were so frantic

to beat their wings in. Science
has no answers. Sometimes, she sits

on the edge of the bed for hours
in the morning silence, waiting.

Honey

Bears   who when awake
are not   become diabetic   it seems
as they hibernate   Scientists think

this is what allows them
to devour their stores of fat
during those long winter sleeps   Do they dream

of test tubes and reagents?   Is there
on the tongue of every sleeping bear
the faintest hint   growing day by day

                                                of sweetness?

Insomnia

The astronaut can't sleep

      The astronaut can't sleep   in zero gravity

           The astronaut can't sleep   in zero gravity   because

                  of

                  floating

              dreams

They weave   and dip like lunar ducks in orbit   She lunges
      for land   but finds no purchase so slips
    into the airlock to be emptied   to be filled   There

is Earth and there   half-way through Earth's night   is Ursa Major

     Eyes wide   awake she waits

        for some speedoflight transmission   a sign

           that the Bear   is listening

Submarine

I'm under water
and there is the sky

and my hair's oil-
slicked and I'm wondering why

I can't stop thinking
of you, and I'm wondering

why the Higgs gives everything mass,
and I'm wondering why we don't have proof

of string theory, supersymmetry
and I'm wondering why we can't

be kinder, make war
extinct, and I'm wondering why but I

will not
sink

or stop
thinking of you.

Jigsawed

If I said   Be mine
    would you hand yourself
        over   piece
            by odd-shaped piece   confess
                lack of logic   loss
            of instruction book   that you
        are not   and will never be
  some pastoral landscape   well fitting
        serene

Or would you
turn away, quickly
mash yourself
together into
some sweet whole,
swing back,
brushing off
stray fragments,
smiling, say:
      This is me
      This is me.

Cultivation

Open a small agriculture
in your head   Plant

in rows   leaving one corner
wild   You will not

control the rain   the sun
When pressure rises   sit
        in
        that
        corner
                        dreaming

Oh My Heart

I listen to a programme
        on the radio
                about a book

about young black men
        in some American
                neighbourhood. On the run

it's called, the book
        and I imagine it's not just
                those young men

that neighbourhood
        where police lurk
                by the schoolyard

18-year-old
        good student
                something we'd pass off

as harmless earns him
        12 months, then
                released, no charge

but school says: Can't return.
        Too old.
                Too late.

        One arrest
        One life
        One year

                of lessons missed
                but something learned.

The Observer Paradox

It takes you a moment to realise
that the man with two boxes of knives
turned away by the wait staff
came to bargain

not stay. You watch him
pause on the threshold, miss
his decision: left or right
as you wonder if this place

is his hundredth today,
or the first, or the fifth. He
pricked the skin of this café
so lightly; likely unseen

by the couples, the chattering
families. Will he appear
in the drawing made
by the child over there

with her father? When he gets home,
boxes intact, will the fact that you
saw him make any difference
at all? What's a poem to a person

with a room full of boxes
and boxes of unsold
and unwanted knives?

Some Nature Is Binding

She does not expect
to be recognised
from one occasion

to the next, feels
her face easily
forgotten, is amazed

when not only her
but something she has
said's remembered. This

chips away at her
conviction of insignificance,
but *ohsoslowly*, like

the ancient lichen she has
read about, which grows
one centimetre every

hundred years. She suspects
neither of them can change
shape or pace, or let go

of what they cling to.

This Too Is Prayer

No, not some lover's
glance, a newborn's grin,
sunset, autumn leaves – but

this: green fluorescent
protein, a molecule
borrowed from the jellyfish

to turn our cells to
glowing dancing
labourers we applaud

as they go about
their daily tasks:
building inspection,

maintenance. Now they
have us to witness
their every act; not just,

of course, benign
construction. Not
just, of course, repair.

But how much better,
though, to see. Better
to no longer be in darkness.

Life Just Swallows You Up

Father dies during the appetizers. Mother
    keeps on eating. How's work? she says. I
      pour more wine. She passes

    just after dessert arrives. Shame,
      says the waiter, poised to whisk
        away her Eton Mess. Leave it, I say

    and sit there, orphaned, staring at both puddings,
      wondering how I'm ever going
        to lift my spoon again.

The Legacy Of Chemistry

Chances are high –
despite the fact that we're
so far from where it was
or perhaps because
this is not Italy, given wind speeds
and so on –

that with every breath, we take
in a molecule of Caesar's
last. And, under the skin

of this too-damn-heavy
iron cooking pot
which I paid so much for
and just can't give away

are the remains
of every meal you made
for me, no matter

how I scrub
and scrub it clean.

After The Man Who Finds A 100-Year-Old Bottle Made By Her Great-Grandfather's Company, With His Name Still On It, Won't Sell It To Her

She dreams she breaks
        into his basement, where he
told her he would keep it
        so the label wouldn't fade. It is
too dark, she cannot find it.

She dreams she sees him
        take it, well insulated,
for a walk along the shore. She tries
        to bargain. He, enraged,
flings it into the waves.

Years later, she dreams she is
        inside it, at the bottom
of the sea. How comfortable, how easy
        she breathes, his great-granddaughter,
no matter it is filled with water.

Nothing Here Is Wild

I am sailing
in my copper-bottomed,

copper-sided boat, although
we are not going

anywhere. But if the walls
fell in, the roof was gone,
and the rain kept on

      and if it didn't matter
that I was naked, my skin
wrinkled, my hair wet

      and if I forgot my need
to eat, to drink, love
and pay my taxes

imagine
      how far
      we might get.